W9-BKT-447

ABeCedarios

Mexican Folk Art ABCs in English and Spanish

Cynthia Weill and K.B. Basseches

Wood Sculptures from **Oaxaca** by
Moisés and Armando Jiménez

the **Armadillo** ❁ el **Armadillo**

the **Buffalo** ✷ el **Búfalo**

the **Coyote** ❋ el **Coyote**

el **Chapulín**

Ch is in the Spanish alphabet only.
the grasshopper

the **Dolphin** • el **Delfín**

the Elephant ✸ el Elefante

the **Flamingo** ✸ el **Flamenco**

the **Gorilla** ❁ el **Gorila**

the**Hippopotamus** ✳ el **Hipopótamo**

the **Iguana** ✳ la **Iguana**

the Jaguar ● el Jaguar

the **Koala** • el **Koala**

the **Lion** ❋ el **León**

la **Ll**ama

Ll is in the Spanish alphabet only.
the llama

the **Monkey** ❋ el **Mono**

the **Nutria** ✺ la **Nutria**

el **Ñu**

Ñ is in the Spanish alphabet only.
the gnu

the **O**celot ✺ el **O**celote

the Penguin ✻ el Pingüino

the **Quetzal** ✤ el **Quetzal**

the **Rat** ✦ la **Rata**

el **zorro**

Rr is not a letter in the Spanish alphabet, but the sound is commonly used.
the fox

the **Snake** ✸ la **Serpiente**

the **Turtle** ✿ la **Tortuga**

the **Unicorn** ✲ el **Unicornio**

the **Vicuna** ❈ la **Vicuña**

the **Wapiti** ✸ el **Wapití**

the **X** ❋ el/la **X**

This is an undiscovered animal. Can you give it a name starting with the letter X?
Este es un animal desconocido. ¿Puedes darle un nombre que empiece con la letra X?

the **Yak** ● el **Yac**

the Zedonk ✴ el Zedonk

The animals in *ABeCedarios* were handmade by the Jiménez family who lives in the state of Oaxaca, Mexico. Brothers Armando and Moisés carved the creatures. Their children Alex, Nancy and Eduardo sanded each one. Then the figures were lovingly painted by their wives, Antonia and Oralia. Armando and Moisés are the grandsons of Manuel Jiménez, founder of the Oaxacan woodcarving tradition. Eighty other families in their town of Arrazola also make woodcarvings.

In 1994, *La Real Academia Española* ruled that the Spanish consonants CH and LL would be alphabetized under C and under L, respectively, and not as separate letters, as in the past.

Dedications

To Jean Hebert and Sylvia Lahvis who planted the seeds for this book many years ago. (CSW)
To John Holm for gifts beyond record; and to Adam Edward Basseches-Holm for being himself. (KBB)

Thanks to

Marlene Kurtz, Mari Haas, Talía González, Augusta González, Ann Levine, Hank Baker, Ruth Borgman, the Boucher, Basseches and Holm families, Jeannie Friedman, Inés Greenburger, Will Scanlan, Myriam Chapman, Xochítl Medina, Graeme Sullivan, Hope Leichter, Patricia Velasco, Jossie O'Neill, Ofelía García, Stephanie Owen, Frances and Stephen Weill, Arden Rothstein, Jane Yolen, Jack Bailey, Joseph Seipel, Irene Vazquez, Pamela Taylor, Stephen Carpenter, Alex Bostic, David Burton, and The Bank Street Writers Lab. And a very special thanks goes to Alejandro Jiménez, Raquel Aragón, Mark Basseches, Dr. Richard Toscan and the School of the Arts, Virginia Commonwealth University for travel funds for this project.

Cover and Book Design by
Sergio A. Gómez

FIRST EDITION   10 9 8 7 6 5 4 3 2
Library of Congress Cataloging-in-Publication Data. Weill, Cynthia. ABeCedarios : Mexican folk art ABCs in English and Spanish / by Cynthia Weill and K.B. Basseches ; animal wood carvings by Moisés and Armando Jiménez. 1st ed. p. cm. ISBN 978-1-933693-13-2 1. Folk art—Mexico. 2. Alphabet in art—Juvenile literature. 3. Alphabet books—Juvenile literature. I. Basseches, K. B. II. Jiménez., Moisés. III. Jiménez., Armando. IV. Title. NK844.W45 2007 745.0972—dc22
2007019441

CINCO PUNTOS PRESS
www.cincopuntos.com
EL PASO, TEXAS